Nuru Life Poems

Written in reflection of the glory of God.

By Neema Penuel

The heavens declare the glory of God; and the firmament sheweth his handywork. Day unto day uttereth speech, and night unto night sheweth knowledge.(Psalm 19:1-2)

Table of Contents

Note

This book is the fourth and part of the scripture and Holy Spirit inspired collection. I pray that you will enjoy reading Nuru Life Poems like I have enjoyed writting them. Shalom.

Glorious God

Glorious God and King of all creation,
You who are wonderfully worthy to be praised,
For in you every living life has its source,
Drawing from the riches of your gracious glory,
Endless like the immense wild wide oceans,
Availed to the millions and millions of living creatures,
So each receives richly from your abundance.

Seen the endless expansive ocean,
Considered its forceful waves as they ran ashore,
Wave after wave carrying with it a latent power,
Hidden within the vibrating roar of the waters,
That sustain millions and millions of life within it,
Just a glimpse of your creative ability Glorious One,
For even a thousand wise words per second cannot
fully describe you.

Excellent Spirit

You said to do all to your glory Glorious God
By the power of your excellent spirit,
But she went out to do in her own power and might,
So she kept missing this true mark of excellence,
No matter how hard she tried,
For she was like a branch of a vine cut off,
Trying to bear fruit in its own power,
Futility and frustration became the result.
She returned to you glorious God,
In mercy you received her
And poured your excellent Spirit in the earthen vessel,
A gift to mark your secure seal upon her,
Teaching her to labour to rest in You,
With a faith in you working through love,
And the fruits of righteousness glorified you God.

Grafted in glory

The Olive that grew wild branches,
Not having been cared for hitherto,
You lovingly took and grafted,
Into a cultivated Olive tree,
So it could be nourished and cared for,
Counted among the bearing blessed,
Indeed grafted in your glory.

What made this wild Olive so special,
That you looked upon it with favour?
Oh glorious God creator of heaven and earth,
For this deed was contrary to nature,
But in your hand nature bowed to divinity,
Like darkness bows to light,
And your glory was seen.

You reign

From early awakening morning to late sleepy evening,
From the magnificent sunrise to the golden sunset,
From the bright dawn to darkening nightfall,
From the star filled night to the cloudy morning sky,
You reign Lord God almighty.

Where can we hide from your loving Spirit,
Where can we stand away from your searching eyes,
Where can we walk from your comforting shadow,
Where can we run from your loving presence,
The earth and all its fullness belongs to you Lord God.

You who knows the beginning from the end,
You who's been before the foundation of the world,
You who's also seen the end in your infinite wisdom,
You who's faithful to fulfil your word in time's fullness
You reign forever good Lord.

Awesome in the small things

Show me a tiny kitten playfully climbing a bush,
And a faithful sleepy dog slumbering by the window,
Or a weaver bird carefully building its nest,
You made them all magnificient God,
Designed them in the beginning of time,
For You are awesome also in the small things.

Look at the ever green grass that habours small life,
Lush with green succulent foliage,
Resisting drought with its inbuilt strength,
And the Kikuyu grass that knows how to wage,
A good fight against weeds with its inbuilt power,
For You are awesome also in the small things.

Awesome in the small wonderful Creator,
Lovingly watching over the work of your hands,
To the tiniest detail like a muster seed,
Working even while we the humanity sleep,
And continuing to sustain life with your breath,
For You are awesome also in the small things.

Eternal

GOD You whose love is ever eternal,
Dwelling in bright light in the high heaven,
Yet near here in this sacred holy altar,
Where this essence presence fills,
Like a sweet discreet fragrance,
Drawn near by the Lamb's blood.
Forever in my soul be magnified and praised!

GOD You whose love is ever eternal,
Comforting those hurting broken hearts,
As they eagerly seek Your presence,
Inhabiting the praises of your people,
Whom you have chosen and cleansed,
By the blood of the Lamb and His word,
Forever in my soul be exalted and praised!

You save

Lord you are the awesome One who saves,
The lost sheep that left your chosen flock,
And wondered off into the wilderness,
Where the voice of the shephered is faint,
And the wind is loud and bossy,
Tossing the lost hither and thither.

Lord you are the awesome One who saves,
And brings back into your chosen flock,
Carrying the lost on your shoulders of love,
Restoring their ability to hear your caring voice,
Instead of the enemy’s voice that once confused,
Building them up in your perfect love.

Reminders

Lord you made night and day,
For you wanted to remind of your faithfullness
Like the night and day keep their place,
To silently speak of your precious covenant,
Lasting forever from generation to generation.

Lord you made an elegant eagle,
Flying swiftly as the whirl wind carries it,
To silently speak of your power to renew,
That in that renewal we may labour,
Not for things which perish but for everlasting ones.

Lord you made the dear,
That pants after water when thirsty,
To remind of the thirst within us,
Which only you can quench for the believer,
Not with earthly well water but with rivers of living
water.

Good shepherd

Lord God you watch over your Herd undetered,
Your love given to the world concerned,
That those who have discerned and returned,
To the flock where you serve to preserve,
May find their place to receive grace,
Like fish find place to swim in the ocean.

Given without measure this treasure,
Love that you poured abroad so generously,
In your herd's hearts without hoarding,
Like the sun shines on all under it,
To help your sheep cleave to you,
Waoh what a good shepherd so treasured!

Inhabits our praises

Glorious Lord thank you forevermore,
For inhabiting our true praises like fish inhabit the sea,
You who are glorious in holiness doing us good,
That we may see the wonders you do,
As we by faith flow in your Spirit.

Gracious Lord thank you forevermore,
For doing wonders greater than our praises,
Like a seedling germinates to life larger than itself,
Becoming a tree with nesting branches for birds of air.
And whose fruit is honey sweet to taste.

Gracious Lord thank you forevermore,
For giving us millions of reasons to praise you,
Continually pouring forth like a river of fresh water,
As we look at your word written and sealed,
And see what the precious blood of Jesus bought for us.

Divine Intervention

Beautiful as dawn that breaks through the darkness,
Timely as the sun is sure to go from east to west,
Sure as the falling rain droplets must wet the earth,
Expected like steep ocean waves that must break,
Responding to your Word with angelic intervention.

Not that we deserved this wonderful salvation,
For sin unrepented separated us from you Saviour,
Like smoke it clouded perception with condemnation,
So we fumbled in the darkness of damnation,
Then we cried out to you Lord in that trouble.

You sent your timely wonderful word,
A light that broke through the cloudy darkness,
Scattering it like whirlwind scatters smoke,
With heavenly beings to fulfil its delivering demand,
Angelic intervention fulfilling your word in Spirit.

Amazed

Amazed at He who never sleeps but keeps,
Kingly yet humbly watching over His sleeping creation,
You, you and you among those whom He loves,
Made verily valuable in Christ,
Like a golden vessel so special in His eyes,
I am amazed and delighted to know Him.

Amazed at He who forgives and gives,
Every thing treasured and good from above,
To the creation that He made,
Even man and woman in His very own image,
Like a lion begets a cub in its own likeliness,
I am amazed and delighted to know Him.

Edifier

You gave me a living language,
Perfectly created for whose use,
To edify and beautify at your will,
Like a broom that swips the room,
Removing dirt that collected within,
A saving Spirit sweeping with miracles of restoration,
Edifying with your living presence so fresh and
beautiful.

Sin in the soul caused cursed wounds,
Affected heartily hearing of your living truth,
Pouring forth lies like a polutted water well,
Halleluya that like a disinfectant Jesus blood cleansed,
Allowing your sent word that wholly healed the soul,
From destruction delivering so perfectly,
Edifying with your living presence so fresh and
beautiful.

Pure Faith

His pure faith found you today,
Not for the many marvellous things you did,
But truly treasured because of Jesus precious blood,
Abit like a new born baby in its mama's arms,
He believed in you unto sure salvation,
What a fearful and faithful Lord He is!

His pure faith found you yesterday,
Before the finished foundation of the world,
Not that you knew him enough to seek Him then,
But like the builder's insight into bricks to use,
He knew you for His preconceived purpose,
What a loving and lively Lord He is!

His pure faith will find you tomorrow,
For He has surely said never to leave nor forsake,
Not for the perfect faith you have in Him following,
But for His pure faith in the righteous One in you,
Lord through whom salvation comes for all who call,
The name of the living Lord that is Jesus Christ,
What a magnificent and mighty Lord He is!

Cleansed in Jesus blood

Lead us away from the nagging noise,
Empty pitiful promises made in desperation,
By the devil daring to speak in darkness,
Into the living light of your cleansing blood and word,
Pure, purging from every sin and its consequences,
That we may magnify your Holy name Lord Jesus,
Like a candle lit in the light of the magnificent sun.

Your cleansing blood was surely shed for us,
And for every believing living being,
That through its cleansing, calming assurance,
We may enter into the holy of holies,
Where we find granted grace to help in times of need,
Deliverance sent from the throne of the Almighty,
Like rain sent to quench the thirst of dry ground.

Peace come

Peace came caring for our minds,
From the sure source of all good things,
The high heaven above where He dwells,
The gracious God who blesses and none can curse,
Like a lamb born cannot return to the womb,
For once out its here for a purpose,
This blessed pure peace is here to stay.

Perfect peace came caring for our minds,
Availed for all whose minds chose security in Him,
Believing in His agape love to prevail,
The loving God above who gives every good thing,
From heavens high like rain to a thirsty ground,
Pouring generously this precious, godly gift,
This blessed pure peace is here to stay.

Everlasting

The Almighty loves with an everlasting love,
See how He calms storms with a timely word,
Spoken with a force mightier than any turbulence,
Entering the root of the storm and stilling it,
For when He speaks all nature hears to obey,
His children who look to Him see and believe,
Who can do what He alone can do.

The Almighty loves with an everlasting love,
See how He speaks grace gently to your heart,
Quieting every storm of life with His Word and Spirit,
Asking you to cast every care to Him who cares,
More than a good earthly father cares for his child,
Yet that care is like candle light compared to Sunlight,
Trully none can do what the Lord alone can do.

You can

Good Lord I cannot but you can,
You can remove this yoke from off my shoulders,
You can give me your light burden and easy yoke,
You can take this care and turn into a good testimony,
You can give me your word which is truth and life.

Good Lord I cannot but you can,
You can deliever him from destruction with one word,
You can nourish his soul with new strength from above,
You can align his will to your word and spirit,
You can prosper his soul and heal his body.

Good Lord I cannot but you can,
You can give us a good word to believe and manifest,
You can change the course of this event by faith in You,
You can make even our enemy to be at peace with us,
You can make our steps sure so we live to glorify you.

These three

Like the shephered that finds the lost sheep,
Is the blood of the lamb sent to save me and you,
Bringing us out of the pit wherein is no water,
Setting us safely on a secure rock,
That we may enjoy fellowship with you God.

Like the iron that sharpens iron,
Is your holy word sent to heal me and you,
Delivering from destruction with accuracy,
Prospering our souls and health therein,
That we may live to praise you good God.

Like the wind that blows away the chaff,
Is your Spirit sent to align me and you to His will,
Sweeping away that which defiles this holy temple,
Making it fit as the abode of a heavenly King,
That in Him we may live now and eternally.

Sun of freedom

Come let us all sing joyfully to the Almighty God,
For freedom came with the valuable price,
So verily valuable that none can afford,
Yet like He who affords more than the sun,
The Lord became our only Sun of freedom,
Giving His life so immensely valuable for ours,
Shine, shine, shine gently upon us.

Let us all dance joyfully to the Almighty God,
For His dear deliverance that freed us,
So perfectly washing us in the precious lamb's blood,
And like the prodigal son who came to find himself,
Only His grace enabled us to find ourselves,
Returning home to dignity in the Sun of freedom,
Shine, shine, shine gently upon us.

Life giver

You glorious God are our life giver,
From the first foundation of the earth,
Living life's breath came from your riches in glory,
You availed this living life to us in Christ,
And to every precious person you persuaded to believe,
Like you make the sun shine on all that are under it,
In believing we are blessed to see your great glory,

In your wonderful word we find light,
This lovely light that shines in darkness,
Without even thick darkness defeating it,
For in it is living life stronger than defeated death,
Having conquered it and placed it under your feet,
Like dawn easily scatters the black of the night,
Lord we believe you and see your great glory.

Protector of Sanity

Thank you loving God precious protector of our sanity,
Giving us the only wholesome hope to hold on to,
In a world swayed hither and tither by uncertainity,
Human doctrines with some natural elements of truth,
But silently shrouded in costly confusion,
That never permanently helped those who coined them.

Thank you loving God precious protector of our sanity,
Giving us your pure precious word to hear and believe,
Imparting vivid visions of what you have promised,
Through your Holy Spirit hovering over that word,
Like in the beginning where earth formless and void,
Became filled with your manifest glorious goodness,
Where sane Adam abode in your absolute abundance.

Thank you loving God precious protector of our sanity,
Instructing us to readily renew our minds,
Washing in your word like feet are washed in water,
For without washing dirt readily accumulates,
Carelessly covering the work of creation beneath,
With a layer never known to benefit the feet,
But burdening with layer after layer of the undesired.

The code of grace

The good scarlet code of grace,
That gracious precious code that brought salvation,
To one poor prostitute and her entire family,
A win sign that ensured destruction passed over them,
Bearing the blessing speaking divine protection,
Rahab lived to see God’s blessed words come to pass,
In a time when things troubled crumbled around her.

The good scarlet code of grace,
Faithful Rahab tied it to the window,
Instructions she had recieved from God’s own spies,
The sure sign of her salvation for her household,
From the most powerful, merciful Lord Living,
Who deemed the life of a faithful prostitute precious,
While many unfaithful nobles received damnation.

You God of hope

You good God of living hope,
Not based on mere hearsay and fairy tales,
Like a bobbly bouncing castle built in air,
But on your sure lively word,
Sealed with your sweet Holy Spirit.

This hope gives a blueprint of forgiveness,
As clear as the milky way on a dark cloudless night,
On what we believers build our faith in God,
Enabling us to forgive like we have been forgiven,
For the God of hope is our light.

Hope as beautiful as the solid golden ring,
Gently embracing the ring finger with assuarance,
That your presence though not visible yet is near,
Waiting to manifest that hope on which we build,
Faith that comes by hearing and hearing God’s word.

Nothing to fear

Nothing to fear here for our God is a consuming fire,
Caring so much that evil fear is kept below His feet,
Defeated like a blade of dry grass lying in the field,
With no power to effect any change to itself,
But be burnt to ash by the consuming fiery fire.

Nothing to fear there for our God is a consuming fire,
That sent His word who healed us who believe,
Oh the joy of timely deliverance from destruction,
Like the appearance of ripe fruit on a date tree,
Satiating the hunger of travellers in the desolate desert.

Nothing to fear there for our God is a consuming fire,
Look and rejoice at how He defeated sad sin,
That one bad thing we mankind inherited from Adam,
Triumping gloriously over it like heaven over earth,
Nothing to fear indeed but look to our caring Christ.

We called

You heard our calling caring loving Lord,
You answered us gracious good Lord,
You directed our paths precious Lord,
You reminded us that we will always be yours,
Your chosen generation of royal preaching priests,
Cleansed by the pure purifying blood of the lamb.

You showed us your perfect Fatherly faithfullness
You gave us your living wonderful word,
You helped us appreciate your every vital virtue,
You made us know the holy hidden mysteries therein,
You manifested your faithfullness in our faith,
We are grateful to be your children gracious good God.

You gently guided us with your eyes,
You spoke a winning word that directed our paths,
You gave us the gracious gift of your presence,
You ensured that our feet faltered not into a snare,
You reminded us of the lamb’s precious pure blood,
That in believing gratitude we may dare draw near You.

Glorious works

We consider the wonderful works of your hands,
Your people whom you chose, cleansed and preserved,
Not by own works but by faith in that perfect peace,
Your lamb that was given graciously to take away sin,
That the world may now know the love and believe.
We worship you living, loving Heavenly Father.

We believe in your precious, pure word dear Lord,
That you gave so your pact people gain insight,
Into the thoughts that you think towards them,
Not of evil but of everlasting, gracious goodness,
The wonderful works of your hands on earth.
We praise your holy, honourable name glorious Lord.

The author

Neema Penuel is a Christian and Afro-Dane who enjoys writing in both non-fiction and creative styles. With a background in the Anglican church where she was baptised and confirmed, Neema later became part of the charismatic-full gospel, where she was baptised in water and in the Holy Spirit. She is active in Christian mission work in partnership with other believers; praying for people's salvation, preaching the gospel in the hope that many more are saved and come to a personal knowledge of Jesus Christ.

Neema holds a doctorate degree in pastoral ministry from Atlantic Seminary Florida, masters in information architecture & multimedia from Aalborg University and a bachelor of science in Agriculture from Nairobi University.

She is married to Jan, an active Christian leader and computer programmer. Together they are raising a Christ centred family.

Publisher: BoD – Copenhagen, Denmark
Printing: BoD – Norderstedt, Germany
ISBN: 978-87-4301-614-4

MIX
Papir fra ansvarlige kilder
Paper from responsible sources
FSC® C105338